Florence Nightingale

History Maker Bios

Susan Bivin Aller

LERNER PUBLICATIONS COMPANY • MINNEAPOLIS

In loving memory of our Flo, Florence Athey Fisher, and her lifetime of caring for Fritz

Text copyright © 2007 by Susan Bivin Aller
Illustrations copyright © 2007 by Lerner Publishing Group, Inc.

Illustrations by Tad Butler

Lerner Publications Company
A division of Lerner Publishing Group, Inc.
241 First Avenue North
Minneapolis, MN 55401 U.S.A.

Website address: www.lernerbooks.com

Library of Congress Cataloging-in-Publication Data

Aller, Susan Bivin.
    Florence Nightingale / Susan Bivin Aller.
       p.   cm. — (History maker bios)
    Includes bibliographical references and index.
    ISBN 978–0–8225–7609–9 (lib. bdg. : alk. paper)
    1. Nightingale, Florence, 1820–1910—Juvenile literature. 2. Nurses—
England—Biography—Juvenile literature. I. Title.
RT37.N5A457 2007
610.73092—dc22 [B]   2006035849

Manufactured in the United States of America
1 2 3 4 5 6 – JR – 12 11 10 09 08 07

TABLE OF CONTENTS

INTRODUCTION

Florence Nightingale lived in England at a time when there were few trained nurses. Ever since childhood, Florence had cared deeply about the sick. As she grew, she felt a calling from God. She believed that God wanted her to improve the care of ill people.

In 1854, Florence took thirty-eight female nurses to serve with her in the Crimean War. It was the first time women had worked in British military hospitals. Florence saw the horrors of war. She decided to devote her life to improving hospitals, nursing, and public health practices.

Florence set new standards for nursing. They helped make it a respectable job for women. She is often called the founder of modern nursing.

This is her story.

1 BORN TO SERVE

Fanny and William Nightingale's second daughter was born on May 12, 1820. They named her Florence, after her birthplace of Florence, Italy. Florence had an older sister who was born a year earlier in Naples, Italy. Her name was Parthenope. That was the old name for Naples. Her family called her Parthe.

When Florence was one year old, the Nightingales went home to England. William owned land and a big country house called Lea Hurst in Derbyshire. He was rich and didn't need to work. He managed his property, studied, and traveled.

Fanny wanted more excitement. She loved to entertain famous artists, writers, and politicians. Fanny talked William into buying another huge house on some land in Hampshire. It was called Embley Park. It was closer to London, where Fanny could have a lively social life.

The Nightingale family spent most of their time at Embley Park (BELOW), but they lived at Lea Hurst in the summer.

Florence and Parthe had governesses to teach them at home. Fanny also kept the girls busy with lessons in music, art, dancing, and needlework. She let them read the Bible and books that gave them information. But she didn't allow storybooks. Fanny wanted her daughters to do well in subjects that would make them good wives and mothers. There was no need to prepare them for careers. In the 1800s, upper-class women rarely had jobs, except for charity work to help the poor or needy.

Fanny Nightingale (CENTER) posed for this portrait with Florence (LEFT) and Parthenope (RIGHT).

DOLL HOSPITAL

When Florence caught whooping cough, she pretended her dolls had it too. She wrapped cloths around their necks. Then she put them to bed in a long row as if they were in a hospital.

Florence didn't like all the guests and parties that swirled around her. She was happier on days when she was sick in bed. Then she could be alone with her daydreams. With her mother, Florence often took soup or clothing to the poor who lived on her family's land. She also sat with the sick or dying.

Florence was smart and well organized. At the age of eight, she began writing her life story—in French! She constantly made lists and charts. They described everything from her flower collection to doses of medicine given to the sick. She kept track of every penny she spent. She wrote long letters and kept a diary. She worried about being good and doing what God wanted.

Florence (LEFT) preferred studying and writing in her journals to the parties that her mother and sister enjoyed.

When Florence was eleven, her father took over her education. Florence loved being with William in his study full of books. Only men could attend universities in those days. But William taught her as much as any young man would have learned at college. He taught Florence mathematics, composition (writing), and history. She learned five languages. She and William discussed philosophy, business, and politics.

Parthe, on the other hand, preferred to be with Fanny and other women. Parthe liked planning parties and visiting friends. She became jealous of Florence, who was smarter and livelier.

When Florence was sixteen, something extraordinary happened to her. "On February 7, 1837, God spoke to me and called me to His service," she wrote. She didn't know exactly what kind of work God wanted her to do. She only knew God had chosen her for something special.

Seven months later, the Nightingales began a long European vacation. Fanny wanted Florence and Parthe to be ready for marriage when they returned. Fanny hoped the trip would improve their manners and broaden their education.

Florence (LEFT) sat for this portrait with Parthe in about 1836.

Florence loved the traveling and sightseeing. She met interesting people and kept detailed records of everything. She made a special study of the work of European hospitals and charities.

When she went back home to England, Florence lived in luxury again. But she was upset by the poverty and illness she saw all around her. She asked a friend what she could do to make a difference. Was God calling her to care for people who were ill? If so, she needed to train to be a nurse.

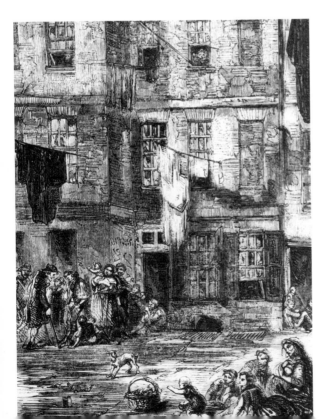

In the 1800s, only poor people went to hospitals. Poor London neighborhoods like this one were crowded, and diseases spread quickly from person to person.

Wealthy people could afford to pay doctors to treat them at home. The doctors might not work in hospitals at all.

Florence asked her parents for permission to study nursing. She said a family friend who was a doctor would train her. Fanny and William refused to allow it. In England at that time, nurses were considered the lowest form of hired help. They had no medical training. Most of them were rough women who were often drunk. They were treated badly by doctors. They got sick from the filth and the diseases in hospitals. Caregivers, Florence wrote, were "merely women who would be servants if they were not nurses. . . . It was as if I had wanted to be a kitchen-maid."

2 BREAKING FREE

Florence felt trapped. She had no money of her own. And even at the age of twenty-five, she couldn't leave home without her family's permission. "I shall never do anything, and am worse than dust and nothing," she wrote to a cousin. For a while, she worked for free at a charity school for poor children in London.

The Nightingales still hoped Florence would marry. To her family's great disappointment, she turned down two proposals of marriage. She believed God had chosen her to be a single woman. But how would she fill her days? "I see so many of my kind who have gone mad for want of something to do," she wrote.

Florence's parents let her travel for several months in Italy, Egypt, and Greece. She went with the Bracebridges, friends of her parents. In Rome, Italy, Florence met Sidney and Liz Herbert. They shared her interest in improving hospitals and training women to be nurses.

Florence turned down a marriage proposal from Richard M. Milnes (RIGHT). He was a poet and a politician.

Florence heard her second call from God while she was in Egypt. She wrote in her diary, "God called me in the morn'g & asked me 'Would I do good for Him, for Him alone without the reputation [fame].'" On her thirtieth birthday in Athens, Greece, she dedicated her life to doing God's will. She vowed there would be "no more childish things . . . no more love, no more marriage."

In the 1800s, the ruins of Karnak, Egypt, were very popular with rich travelers.

Each day, the Kaiserswerth deaconesses crossed Basilica Square (ABOVE). It lay between the church and hospital.

Then one of Florence's prayers was answered. The Bracebridges let Florence spend two weeks at the Kaiserswerth Institution of Deaconesses in Germany. They did not tell her father and mother. Protestant nurses, or deaconesses, trained and worked at Kaiserswerth's hospital, orphanage, and school. After two weeks, Florence became certain of her calling. She was to make changes in how nurses were trained and hospitals were organized in England.

Parthe liked drawing, and she became an excellent artist. She sketched this portrait of Florence and her pet owl, Athena, around 1850.

When she returned home in August, Florence faced an angry family. They had found out about Kaiserswerth. Parthe was so upset she had a nervous breakdown. Florence's parents insisted she stay home and keep Parthe company. Once again, Florence attended parties and entertained endless visitors. She was miserable.

The only bright spot in that period was her new friendship with Elizabeth Blackwell. Elizabeth was the first woman doctor in the United States. She had come to London to study. Elizabeth's family had encouraged and supported her career from the start. Unfortunately, Florence's family still controlled her life.

Elizabeth Blackwell

Dr. Elizabeth Blackwell moved to the United States with her English parents when she was eleven. After graduating from medical school in New York, she trained in Paris and London. In 1857, she opened the New York Infirmary for Women and Children. During the U.S. Civil War (1861–1865), she arranged for women nurses to serve in military hospitals.

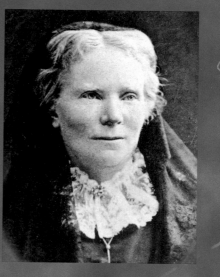

At last, Florence's parents gave in and let her return to Kaiserswerth for three months of training. She put on the simple blue print dress worn by deaconesses and started working in the hospital and orphanage. She saw how a hospital was run. She learned how important it was to teach the nurses their duties. She saw the results of discipline, organization, and routines. Florence believed that nursing was more than a simple job. It was a calling from God that women could be proud to do.

In the rest of Europe, many nurses were Catholic nuns. These German nuns are helping wounded soldiers in a field hospital.

After Kaiserswerth, Florence found that her family continued to be upset with her. However, friends had urged them to let Florence have a career. Finally, her father agreed, even though her mother and Parthe still opposed. He decided to give Florence an allowance of five hundred pounds a year, a very generous amount. With that, she could afford to move away from home and do what she wished.

3 OFF TO WAR

Florence's career began with an offer
from her friend Liz Herbert. A nursing
home for women in London needed a
superintendent. Liz Herbert asked Florence to
take the job. Florence would not receive a
salary. It was not proper for a lady to work for
a salary. But it didn't matter. At age thirty-
three, Florence finally had freedom from her
family. She also had a hospital to manage.

Florence had the training and ability to run the institution well. Many of her skills came from helping with her family's large houses and lands. She knew how to save money when purchasing medicines and supplies. She raised standards of cleanliness and insisted that the hospital serve healthy food. She organized the nurses to improve the care of patients.

At the end of one year, Florence felt her work at the nursing home was done. She wanted to move on. She applied to become superintendent of nursing at King's College Hospital in London. Florence planned to start a nursing school there that would be similar to Kaiserswerth.

King's College Hospital was a training hospital where medical students studied with working doctors.

Suddenly, world events changed everything. Great Britain entered the Crimean War (1853–1856) against Russia. British soldiers were sent to fight far away in the Crimean Peninsula on the Black Sea. That area was part of Russia then. The *Times* newspaper of London reported horrifying conditions among the sick and wounded in the Crimea. They had almost no medicine, food, or other supplies.

William Howard Russell (LEFT) was a reporter for the Times. He spent almost two years living with the army and reporting on the Crimean War.

Sidney Herbert (RIGHT) worked hard to improve health conditions for soldiers in Great Britain and India.

Florence's friend Sidney Herbert was Secretary at War in the British government. His office was responsible for taking care of the soldiers. But the army had no clear system for ordering and moving supplies. Many departments were in charge of supporting the army. And no one knew who had the final say.

British soldiers in the Crimea faced cold, wet weather that made it hard to stay healthy.

The *Times* articles outraged the British people. Something had to be done and quickly. Then Sidney Herbert had a brilliant idea. He and Florence had often talked of having women nurses help care for the soldiers in military hospitals. Herbert wrote Florence to ask if she would take a group of female nurses to the Crimea. This would show that Great Britain cared for its soldiers. "There is but one person in England that I know of who would be capable of organizing . . . such a scheme," Herbert wrote to her.

Florence was way ahead of Herbert. She had already written a letter asking to be sent to the Crimea with nurses. Her letter crossed in the mail with his! Florence accepted Herbert's offer at once. It took her only a week to select nurses, have uniforms made, and collect supplies.

On October 21, 1854, Florence and thirty-eight nurses crossed the English Channel to France. They were met by cheering crowds who had heard about the brave group.

Florence designed nurses' uniforms with hats and sashes. This nurse's sash bears the name of the hospital at which she worked.

Newspapers reported every day on Florence's activities. People were fascinated that Miss Nightingale, "a young, graceful, feminine, rich, and popular" lady, was going to nurse the soldiers. The British had never had women nurses in military hospitals. With the war becoming a national disaster, the public longed for a hero—or better yet, a heroine. Florence Nightingale filled that role. The *Times* asked for donations to support her. Money and goods poured in.

Sick and wounded soldiers crowd into boats after a battle. Some soldiers had to sail for several days to reach a hospital.

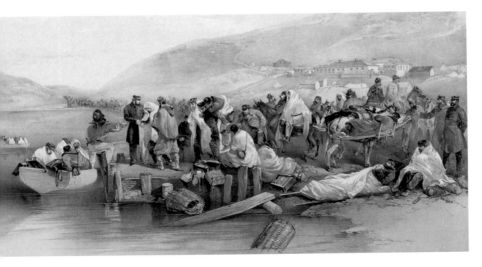

Florence's group sailed across the Mediterranean Sea from Marseilles, France, on October 27. They landed nine days later at Constantinople in the Ottoman Empire. (This city is modern-day Istanbul, Turkey.) They were lowered into small boats and rowed across the Bosporus Strait to Scutari. Two hospitals for the British army were in that town. Both hospitals were overflowing with the sick and wounded.

Conditions were even worse than anyone had imagined! Men had been sent three hundred miles from the battlefields across the Black Sea. Some had lain on the decks of ships for two weeks with little or no medical attention. Many had diseases such as dysentery, cholera, and typhus.

The hospitals had few beds or medical supplies. They were filthy and filled with fleas, lice, and rats. The stench was terrible. Clogged sewer pipes lay beneath the hallways. The toilets overflowed, and no one emptied the chamber pots that men also used as toilets. There were no vessels to carry water. The food was often spoiled. It could scarcely be chewed or swallowed.

Soldiers who were too weak to walk had to use chamber pots instead of toilets.

At first, the doctors at Scutari refused to let Florence and her nurses care for patients. They were annoyed that this high-society woman and her nurses had been sent to help them. But a few days after Florence arrived, five hundred wounded men came from the battlefields. At least one thousand more were on the way. The overwhelmed doctors asked the nurses to begin their work.

CHARGE OF THE LIGHT BRIGADE

A great disaster of the Crimean War took place only a week before Florence and her nurses arrived. It was the Charge of the Light Brigade during the Battle of Balaclava. Nearly 670 British soldiers on horseback charged into a trap. They were met by Russian gunfire on nearly all sides. More than 100 men died. *Times* reporter William Howard Russell wrote an eyewitness account of the event.

4 LADY WITH THE LAMP

Florence ordered a thorough cleaning of the hospital. She insisted chamber pots be emptied regularly. Florence told her nurses to make mattress bags and stuff them with clean straw. She gave them to the sick and wounded who had been lying on bare floors.

Florence worked miracles with supplies she bought with the *Times* Crimea Fund money. She bought healthy food that her nurses prepared for the weakest men. She bought fabric to make bandages, pillows, and shirts. When the army ran out of medicine, her supply saved many lives.

Back in England, Sidney Herbert kept sending supplies. But not all arrived. A hurricane sank one of the biggest ships. Others were delayed in ports because no one had the authority to release them. Some even went to the wrong ports!

There were two hospital buildings at Scutari. The Barrack Hospital (BELOW LEFT) opened when the first building was full.

Most of the doctors resented Florence's help. But the soldiers worshipped her. Every night, she walked alone through the long hallways lined with beds. She carried a small lamp that glimmered in the dark. The men felt her gentle, healing presence. She spoke quietly or laid her hand on them. She stayed at the bedsides of the dying men.

An artist painted Florence as the lady with the lamp visiting a wounded soldier.

Florence inspects one of the new rooms at Scutari.

Florence's greatest problem was that the death rate in the Barrack Hospital remained so high. She had done all she could to clean the hospital and care for the men. Yet more of her patients died than did those in field hospitals, near the battlefront.

In February 1855, the British government sent a group to investigate. They discovered that sewer gases from the clogged drains under the hospital were poisoning the men. When the drains were cleared, the death rate dropped quickly.

One of Florence's tasks was to write letters for soldiers who were too weak to move. She also wrote to the families of soldiers who had died in her hospital.

In May 1855, Florence sailed across the Black Sea to visit field hospitals in the Crimea. Two weeks later, she fell ill with a very high fever. She was not able to work again until late summer.

When she recovered, she tried to find ways to improve the lives of the wounded soldiers and raise their spirits. She set up reading rooms and recreation programs. She arranged for the men to send money home to their families, instead of wasting it on gambling or drinking.

Florence treated the soldiers with respect and sympathy. Until then, they had been thought of in the same way as female nurses—lower class, ignorant, and of no importance except to do their duty.

The Crimean War ended with the Treaty of Paris, signed on March 30, 1856. Florence continued her hospital work in the Crimea until July. Then she went home to her family. She was thin and worn out. She looked much older than her thirty-six years.

In this picture from 1856, Florence still looks tired from her work in the Crimea.

Finding out that she was a national heroine made her very uncomfortable. Baby girls were being named Florence in her honor. So were ships and even racehorses! Poems and songs praised her. The Nightingales were thrilled with her fame. They wanted her to accept invitations to speak and to attend parades and parties in her honor. But Florence was exhausted. She wanted time alone. She refused, as she had before, to play the role of the society lady.

Something else haunted Florence. It was the faces of the dying men at Scutari Barrack Hospital. If only she had known that poisonous sewer gases were killing them. But it was too late.

5 "I FIGHT THEIR CAUSE"

"I stand at the altar of the murdered men, and while I live I fight their cause," Florence wrote in a private note. She believed that it was her God-given duty to change the health-care system of the British army. She pushed her friends in government to make changes so that nothing like the Crimean tragedy would ever happen again.

Florence spent weeks at Parthe's country home, Claydon House. She worked on reports in this room.

Florence never fully recovered from the fever she caught in the Crimea. She did not leave her bed for weeks. She and her family thought she might die soon. However, being ill allowed her to work alone in her room. And work she did! She turned out hundreds of pages of reports, recommendations, statistics, and charts.

She also demanded much work from her friends. Many of them were important men in the government. She worked them to the point of exhaustion and illness, yet she outlived most of them!

Years passed, and Florence's influence spread. One by one, her ideas were adopted. She became Britain's top expert on public health. Authorities in India sought her advice. She helped make changes in India's health care and living conditions.

In 1860, the Nightingale Training School for Nurses opened in London. Florence took pride in her nurses. The Nightingale method of nursing spread to many countries, including the United States.

American friends asked Florence for help during the U.S. Civil War. She sent private advice and reports that helped both sides improve their military medical services.

In 1886, Florence (CENTER) invited nurses from London hospitals to visit with her at Claydon House.

Over the years, Florence lived a very private life. She spent most of her time in her bedroom and rarely received visitors. She wrote volumes of reports and letters, and she continued to give advice on public health issues in Britain. She was doing the work she felt God had called her to do.

At the age of eighty-seven, Florence received the Order of Merit. She was the first woman to be so honored. By this time, her eyesight and her memory were failing. But when the medal was brought to her, she still knew something special had occurred. "Too kind," she murmured, "too kind."

In this picture from 1898, Florence holds some of the letters and reports that kept her busy during years of illness.

VISITING THE QUEEN

After the Crimean War, Queen Victoria and Prince Albert invited Florence to visit them at Balmoral Castle in Scotland. Florence's ideas on hospital reform impressed them. "Such a head! I wish we had her at the War Office," wrote the queen. Later, the queen offered Florence an apartment in Kensington Palace, but Florence turned it down.

Florence Nightingale died August 13, 1910. She was ninety years old. Her coffin was carried by soldiers whose units had fought in the Crimean War. She was buried next to her parents near her childhood home.

Florence's work changed the way people thought about soldiers and nurses. For the first time, men who chose to become soldiers were treated with respect. And trained women nurses were valued. Florence's lifelong work in health care, nursing education, and hospital planning improved the lives of people everywhere.

TIMELINE

In the year . . .

1821   she and her family went to live in England.

1829   she began writing her life story in French.   `Age 8`

1831   she began studying at home with her father as teacher.

1837   Florence heard her first call from God.   `Age 16`

1838   she and her family traveled in Europe.

1850   Florence heard her second call from God.   `Age 29`

1851   she trained at Kaiserswerth in Germany.

1852   Florence heard God call her to be "a savior."

1853   she became superintendent of a charity hospital in London.

1854   she led thirty-eight nurses to serve in the Crimean War.   `Age 34`

1856   she returned to England and was hailed as a hero.

1860   she opened the Nightingale Training School for Nurses.

1865   Florence moved to her own house in London.   `Age 45`

1907   King Edward VII awarded her the Order of Merit.

1910   she died on August 13.   `Age 90`

"Santa Filomena"

In 1857, the American poet Henry Wadsworth Longfellow wrote a poem called "Santa Filomena" (daughter of light) to honor Florence Nightingale. Here are some lines from the poem.

Honor to those whose words or deeds
Thus help us in our daily needs . . .

Thus thought I, as by night I read
Of the great army of the dead,
The trenches cold and damp,
The starved and frozen camp,—

The wounded from the battle-plain,
In dreary hospitals of pain,
The cheerless corridors,
The cold and stony floors.

Lo! In that house of misery
A lady with a lamp I see
Pass through the glimmering gloom,
And flit from room to room. . . .

A lady with a lamp shall stand
In the great history of the land,
A noble type of good,
Heroic womanhood.

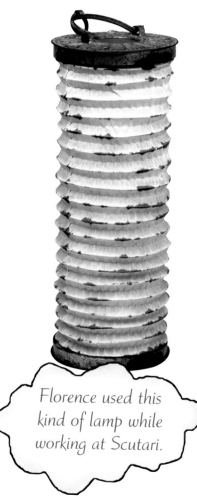

Florence used this kind of lamp while working at Scutari.

FURTHER READING

Bachrach, Deborah. *The Charge of the Light Brigade.* San Diego: Lucent Books, 1997. Read the dramatic story of the Battle of Balaclava in 1854.

Bachrach, Deborah. *The Crimean War.* San Diego: Lucent Books, 1998. This is an easy-to-read account of the Crimean War.

Baker, Rachel. *The First Woman Doctor: The Story of Elizabeth Blackwell, M.D.* New York: Scholastic, 1971. Read this biography of the struggles and achievements of the first woman doctor in the United States.

Gorrell, Gena K. *Heart and Soul: The Story of Florence Nightingale.* Toronto: Tundra, 2000. This biography shows Nightingale's drive and determination and how she became known as the Lady with the Lamp.

Ransom, Candice. *Clara Barton.* Minneapolis: Lerner Publications Company, 2003. This book tells the story of the woman who aided wounded soldiers during the U.S. Civil War and founded the American Red Cross.

WEBSITES

The Florence Nightingale Museum
http://www.florence-nightingale.co.uk/
This is the official website of the Florence Nightingale Museum in London.

Showcases—Voices of History: Florence Nightingale
http://www.bl.uk/onlinegallery/themes/voices/nightingale.html
Listen to a recording made by Florence Nightingale in 1890.